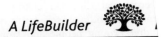

CHRISTIAN LEADERSHIP

9 studies
for individuals or groups

John Stott

with Carolyn Nystrom

With Notes for Leaders

Scripture Union is an international Christian charity working with churches in more than 130 countries providing resources to bring the good news about Jesus Christ to children, young people and families – and to encourage them to develop spiritually through the Bible and prayer. As well as coordinating a network of volunteers, staff and associates who run holidays, church-based events and school Christian groups, Scripture Union produces a wide range of publications and supports those who use their resources through training programmes.

Scripture Union, 207–209 Queensway, Bletchley, MK2 2EB, UK.
e-mail: info@scriptureunion.org.uk
www.scriptureunion.org.uk

Scripture Union Australia: Locked Bag 2, Central Coast Business Centre, NSW 2252.
www.su.org.au

ISBN 978 1 84427 691 2

First published in the United States by InterVarsity Press 2009.
Published in Great Britain by Scripture Union 2012.

This study guide is based on and adapted from Basic Christian Leadership ©2002 by John Stott.

Printed in India by Thomson Press India Ltd.

Contents

Getting the Most Out of
Christian Leadership

A leader, according to the simplest definition, is someone who commands a following. To lead is to go ahead, to show the way and inspire other people to follow. Leaders are needed in every walk of life; leadership is not restricted to politicians, the opinion-formers who dominate the media and the senior executives of multinational companies. Leaders can also be influential in their local communities: teachers in the school, students in the university, parents in the home and in many other ways.

Leadership is a word shared by Christians and non-Christians alike, but this does not mean that their concept of leadership is the same. On the contrary, Jesus introduced the world to a new style of servant-leadership. He said:

> You know that those who are regarded as rulers of the Gentiles lord it over them, and their high officials exercise authority over them. Not so with you. Instead, whoever wants to become great among you must be your servant, and whoever wants to be first must be slave of all. (Mark 10:42-44)

The most influential leader in the early church was undoubtedly the apostle Paul. Appointed by Jesus as the apostle to the Gentiles, he never lost God's vision of one new humanity—Jews and Gentiles together—for which Paul suffered painful opposition and imprisonment. And in his letters we watch him exercising his leadership skills.

Of course, there are no apostles in the church today who have authority comparable to that of the apostle Paul. Nevertheless, Jesus Christ evidently intended from the beginning that his church should be shepherded, or have pastoral guidance. So from the first missionary journey onward, Paul appointed elders in every church (Acts

14:23), and he later instructed Timothy and Titus to do the same, giving specifications as to what kind of people leaders of Christ's church should be (1 Timothy 3:1-13; Titus 1:5-9).

In the first four chapters of 1 Corinthians, Paul responds to a complex Corinthian situation and to the questions the Corinthians have addressed to him. He does so with admirable clarity, wisdom, humility, love and gentleness: pastoral qualities that are sorely needed by Christian leaders today.

Reading First Corinthians
Owing to its political opposition to Rome, Corinth was destroyed in 146 B.C. Around a hundred years later, it was rebuilt and refounded as a Roman colony by Julius Caesar. It owed its distinction mainly to its strategic location on the narrow Corinthian isthmus. Here it commanded the trade routes both between north and south by land, and east and west by sea. Therefore, it was both a manufacturing and a trading center. It also played host to the world-famous Isthmian Games, which were held in its huge stadium every two years.

Corinth was also a religious city, honoring "many 'gods' and many 'lords,'" as Paul wrote (1 Corinthians 8:5). Among its idolatrous buildings was the temple of Aphrodite, which dominated the Acrocorinth and rose nearly two thousand feet behind the city, and the temple of Apollo in the town center. At the same time Corinth was an immoral city, so that Aristophanes coined the verb "to corinthianize," meaning "to live a licentious life."

Corinth also had political importance as the capital city of the Roman province of Achaia (southern Greece). Thus Corinth was a busy, thriving, affluent, proud and permissive city. Merchants and sailors, pilgrims and athletes, tourists and prostitutes jostled one another in its narrow streets.

Yet in this heathen city there lived a small group of people whom Paul called "the church of God in Corinth," the divine community in the human community. It was a fragrant flower growing in and out of the smelly mud.

Paul had a close, longstanding, personal and pastoral relationship with the Corinthian church. It began in A.D. 50, during his second missionary journey, when he first visited the city and founded its church (2 Corinthians 10:14). Using the three metaphors that he himself developed in these chapters, we may say that he planted the church, while Apollos and others did the watering (1 Corinthians 3:6); he laid the foundation, while others erected the superstructure (3:10); he fathered the church, while others were its guardians and tutors (4:14-15). Over the years Paul visited Corinth at least three times and wrote to its church at least four times, although only two of his letters have survived.

For more than forty years I have been fascinated and challenged by the early chapters of 1 Corinthians. They have cast their spell over me. I believe they have a special message for Christian leaders today, whether ordained or not, ministering both inside and outside the church. More of my teaching on this section of Scripture can be found in *Basic Christian Leadership*, which makes an excellent companion to these studies.

Suggestions for Individual Study

1. As you begin each study, pray that God will speak to you through his Word.

2. Read the introduction to the study and respond to the personal reflection question or exercise. This is designed to help you focus on God and on the theme of the study.

3. Each study deals with a particular passage so that you can delve into the author's meaning in that context. Read and reread the passage to be studied. The questions are written using the language of the New International Version, so you may wish to use that version of the Bible. The New Revised Standard Version is also recommended.

4. This is an inductive Bible study, designed to help you discover for yourself what Scripture is saying. The study includes three types of questions. *Observation* questions ask about the basic facts: who, what, when, where and how. *Interpretation* questions delve into the meaning of the passage. *Application* questions help you discover the implications of the text for growing in Christ. These three keys unlock the treasures of Scripture.

Write your answers to the questions in the spaces provided or in a personal journal. Writing can bring clarity and deeper understanding of yourself and of God's Word.

5. It might be good to have a Bible dictionary handy. Use it to look up any unfamiliar words, names or places.

6. Use the prayer suggestion to guide you in thanking God for what you have learned and to pray about the applications that have come to mind.

7. You may want to go on to the suggestion under "Now or Later," or you may want to use that idea for your next study.

Suggestions for Members of a Group Study

1. Come to the study prepared. Follow the suggestions for individual study mentioned above. You will find that careful preparation will greatly enrich your time spent in group discussion.

2. Be willing to participate in the discussion. The leader of your group will not be lecturing. Instead, he or she will be encouraging the members of the group to discuss what they have learned. The leader will be asking the questions that are found in this guide.

3. Stick to the topic being discussed. Your answers should be based on the verses which are the focus of the discussion and not on outside authorities such as commentaries or speakers. These studies focus on a particular passage of Scripture. Only rarely should you refer to other portions of the Bible. This allows for everyone to participate in in-depth study on equal ground.

4. Be sensitive to the other members of the group. Listen attentively when they describe what they have learned. You may be surprised by their insights! Each question assumes a variety of answers. Many questions do not have "right" answers, particularly questions that aim at meaning or application. Instead the questions push us to explore the passage more thoroughly.

When possible, link what you say to the comments of others. Also, be affirming whenever you can. This will encourage some of the more hesitant members of the group to participate.

5. Be careful not to dominate the discussion. We are sometimes so eager to express our thoughts that we leave too little opportunity for others to respond. By all means participate! But allow others to also.

6. Expect God to teach you through the passage being discussed and through the other members of the group. Pray that you will have an enjoyable and profitable time together, but also that as a result of the study you will find ways that you can take action individually and/or as a group.

7. Remember that anything said in the group is considered confidential and should not be discussed outside the group unless specific permission is given to do so.

8. If you are the group leader, you will find additional suggestions at the back of the guide.

1

Seeing Gifting in God's Imperfect People

1 Corinthians 1:1-9

The image of the church as presented in the first four chapters of 1 Corinthians is extremely ambiguous. There is a paradox at the heart of the church. It is the painful tension between what the church *claims* to be and what it *seems* to be; between the divine ideal and the human reality; between the romantic talk about "the bride of Christ" and the very unromantic, ugly, unholy and quarrelsome Christian community we know ourselves to be. It is the tension between our final, glorious destiny in heaven and our present, very inglorious performance on earth. This is the ambiguity of the church—and it creates a challenge for us as leaders.

GROUP DISCUSSION. What are some of your hopes for your own church?

PERSONAL REFLECTION. Consider your own role within your church. How is your church a more appropriate "bride of Christ" because of your presence?

It's hard to write a letter to a troubled church—but the apostle Paul rose to that challenge. *Read 1 Corinthians 1:1-9.*

1. If these words were written to your own church, what would cause you to read further?

2. Paul begins his letter to the Corinthians by describing himself as "called to be an apostle of Christ Jesus by the will of God" (v. 1). What difference did that make in Paul's leadership?

Think about your own call to leadership. What difference does it make in your own leadership to remember that God was the one who called you into your role?

3. As you examine the wording of this passage, what connections do you see between Paul, the church at Corinth and God?

4. Look more carefully at Paul's description of the church in verse 2 and his hopes expressed in verse 8. What would you expect to find in a letter that opens with these ideals?

5. What would have to happen in your own church if it were to be "blameless on the day of our Lord Jesus Christ" (v. 8)?

6. Focus more carefully on verses 4-7. What assets were already present in the church of Corinth and what were the sources of these assets?

7. What skills, gifts, talents, interests or abilities do you see in your own church? (Consider spiritual as well as practical gifts—or the blending of these.)

8. What does this collection of gifts in your church suggest about potential ministries that God may be equipping your church to do?

9. Look again at verses 2 and 9, and notice several forms of togetherness. How can these various connections strengthen the church?

10. What personal encouragement do you take from God's character and his actions as described in verse 9?

Read aloud 1 Corinthians 1:2, 9, inserting the name of your own church in verse 2. On behalf of your church, pray your thanks, confession, fears and hopes.

Now or Later

Paul spoke of the church in Corinth as called to be "sanctified," "holy," "blameless"—necessary goals for all churches. Yet, as his letter later reveals, the church at Corinth had a long way to go in reaching those goals. What are some areas that your own church needs to address as you travel the road toward being sanctified, holy and blameless in God's sight? How might you become a part of the process? (Make notations in the chart below to guide your thinking.)

My Local Church

Gifts/Skills	Mission/Purpose	Needs	My Role

2

Bringing Unity in the Midst of Division

Passionate believers are a great asset to the Christian church, but they have one frequent flaw. They tend to polarize—and draw others into their various magnetic fields. If that happens often and about matters of import, the frequent flaw becomes fatal. A church can die—and its ministry then becomes lost to those who might have been led to Christ.

GROUP DISCUSSION. What sort of things have you seen Christians divide over? With what results?

PERSONAL REFLECTION. Consider your own role among Christians. When has what you have said or done created unnecessary discord? How are you *now* working toward unity in your church? Pray about these areas as you begin this section of Paul's letter to the church at Corinth.

Paul wrote his letter to *"the* church of God" in Corinth" (v. 2). Yet this single church was probably made up of a number of small house churches—and they were at war with one another. Division seems to come naturally to us; unity is hard. *Read 1 Corinthians 1:10-17.*

1. Imagine and then describe several scenes that may have taken place in the church at Corinth. (Draw on what you know of human nature, the first-century church and Paul's words thus far in his letter.)

2. Focus more intently on verse 10. What do you find here that could begin to heal Corinthian divisions?

3. Why do you think Paul emphasizes a unity of "mind and thought"?

4. Consider a current conflict between Christians. What changes do you think would take place if each person involved in the conflict would say with thoughtful commitment to who Jesus is and how he lived, "I follow Christ"?

5. Read verses 12-13 again. Why do you think the Corinthians were divided over who to follow?

What do you think Paul was trying to communicate through his three rhetorical questions?

6. Look more carefully at verses 14-17. Baptism is important to Christians. It is part of Jesus' Great Commission to his disciples, and Paul gives it strong emphasis in Romans 6:1-4. Why then do you think he speaks so casually about baptism to the Corinthians?

7. How might conflict between Christians over which leader to follow cause "the cross of Christ [to] be emptied of its power" (v. 17)?

8. Bring to mind someone in your church who you find difficult to get along with as a brother or sister. What do you think the apostle Paul would say to you?

9. John Chrysostom (A.D. 347-407) wrote in regard to this text, "Paul keeps nailing them to the name of Christ." How might you begin to nail Christians who are under your influence to the name of Christ— and not your own?

10. Take a few moments to examine your own mind and thoughts (v. 10) as you consider some form of Christian disunity in your own setting. When have you mentally taken a side that is favorable to your own interests?

Where have you quietly hoped that your own name might be looked on with favor?

How could you refocus your mind and your thoughts toward the kind of unity described in this passage?

Pray for two different people on opposite sides of the same conflict.

Now or Later

Paul elsewhere uses strong images to portray Christian unity within the church. The church is "God's field" (1 Corinthians 3:8-9), "God's temple" (1 Corinthians 3:16-17), "the body of Christ" (1 Corinthians 12; Romans 12). The church is "one family" because there is only "one Father," "one Spirit," "one Lord." We share one faith, hope and baptism (Ephesians 4:1-6).

Select one of the unity passages above and prayerfully read it aloud. Ask God to remind you of a situation where the principles of this passage might create unity out of division among God's people. Pray for individual people on both sides of that conflict. Consider if there is something you can do to lead these people away from division and toward spiritual unity. You might find the following sequence to be of help:

Confrontation
Confession
Forgiveness
Reconciliation

3

Finding Power in Weakness

1 Corinthians 1:18-25

We see thirst for power everywhere—in politics and public life, in civil conflict and the resort to arms, in big business and industry, in the professions in which professional expertise threatens those without it, and in primitive societies in which the shaman or witch doctor trades secret power for money.

Unfortunately, we see the same power-hunger in the church: in top-level ecclesiastical power struggles, in denominational disputes, in parachurch organizations that dream of expanding into world empires, in some local churches driven by market forces and others in which the clergy hold all the reins of power and refuse to share it with the laypeople (especially the youth), and even in the pulpit, which is an exceedingly dangerous place for any child of Adam to occupy.

Power! It is more intoxicating than alcohol, more addictive than drugs.

GROUP DISCUSSION. Why is power attractive to so many people?

PERSONAL REFLECTION. In what settings do you find a wrong use of power most tempting?

God's picture of power is not what many of us would paint for ourselves. *Read 1 Corinthians 1:18-25.*

1. What words and ideas do you find paired in this passage that most people would not put together?

2. What questions does this passage raise in your mind?

3. Focus more carefully on verses 18-19. Paul speaks of two different groups of people. Describe each. (What is happening for each group? Why? What seems to be the dividing point?)

4. Reread verses 20-21. How is God's view of wisdom and foolishness different from the ordinary use and understanding of those words?

5. Verses 22-24 speak of three different demonstrations of power. What is appealing or off-putting about each?

6. A crucified Messiah was a contradiction in terms. To Jewish minds, it united two opposite concepts. *Messiah* meant power and triumph. *Crucifixion* meant weakness, humiliation, defeat. How would you try to explain to a Jew of the New Testament era what Paul might mean by the power of the weakness of the cross?

7. What do you think a Christian leader would look like today if he or she exercised the kind of power found in the weakness of the cross?

8. What are some danger signs you see in yourself that show you when you are headed toward a wrong form of power?

9. Paul told the Corinthians, "God was pleased . . . to save those who believe . . . whom God has called, both Jews and Greeks" (vv. 21, 24). What does this suggest to you about God's power?

10. Select one area where you are most likely to be tempted to abuse power: home, workplace, neighborhood, school, church, marriage, parenting. How could you begin to live out the power of the weakness of the cross in that setting?

Pray for those who are in your care in the setting you have described above.

Now or Later

Create a layout of these eight verses that visually shows how words and phrases relate to each other. Use this layout to see and then mark connections throughout the text and to highlight important subjects. What fresh meanings and relationships do you see? The sample below gives you a start.

>**1 Corinthians 1:18-25**
>For the message of the cross is foolishness
>>to those who are perishing,
>
>but
>>to us who are being saved
>>>it is the **power** of God.

4

Placing Confidence in Christ

1 Corinthians 1:26—2:5

In 1958, I was privileged to lead an eight-day mission at the University of Sydney, Australia. On the last night, the meeting was due to be held in the imposing great hall of the university. But I had caught what the Australians call a "wog" (flu bug), which had deprived me of speech. Shortly before the meeting some student leaders gathered around me, and one of them read the words of Jesus to Paul: "My grace is sufficient for you, for my power is made perfect in weakness." Paul continued, "Therefore I will boast all the more gladly about my weaknesses, so that Christ's power may rest on me. . . . For when I am weak, then I am strong" (2 Corinthians 12:9-10). Then the students prayed that these words might be fulfilled in me that night.

The hall was packed. But I could only croak my address into the microphone in monotone, unable to assert my personality or modulate my voice in any way. When the time came for the invitation, however, there was an immediate and eager response. I have been back to Australia ten times since then, and every time someone accosts me somewhere, asking, "Do you remember that meeting in the great hall of Sydney University when you lost your voice? I came to Christ that night."

GROUP DISCUSSION. What would you most likely be thinking if you stepped up to a microphone knowing that you were unable to speak?

PERSONAL REFLECTION. What do you see as one of your most important tasks in the next five to ten years? What are some of your hopes
and fears about that task?

Confidence is not always an asset—especially if that confidence is
misplaced. *Read 1 Corinthians 1:26—2:5.*

1. Suppose you were now faced with one of the most important tasks
of your life. What would you find in this passage that encourages
you?

2. In view of Paul's description of the Corinthians in 1:26-30, what
kinds of people would you expect to see in the church of Corinth?

Based on these verses, do you think Jesus is mostly for the poor and
the weak, or is it important to take the gospel to elite groups—like
students and professional people—too? Explain.

3. Focus on the way Jesus is described in 1:30. What does this convey
about the person and work of Jesus?

4. What is dangerous about boasting—even silently to yourself?

5. Bring to mind one of your latest great accomplishments. What skills and opportunities has God given you that allowed this to happen?

How might your thinking and speaking of this subject become a "boast in the Lord" rather than a boast about yourself?

6. Examine the text again and look for two uses of the phrase "so that." From these, what can you conclude about God's purposes in the way he allowed Christian faith to develop at Corinth?

7. Review Paul's description of himself and his preaching in 2:1-5. Do you think he would be well-received as a guest speaker at your church? Why or why not?

8. What weaknesses of yours made you feel inadequate when you were first called into leadership?

How have you seen the Spirit work through your leadership despite those weaknesses?

9. How might you become a better leader in your own setting, because of this section of Paul's letter to Corinth?

Paul said to the Corinthian Christians, "Let him who boasts boast in the Lord." Consider all God has done that is worth boasting about. Then pray your "boast in the Lord."

Now or Later

Prayerfully meditate on the Scripture text below, Jeremiah's message from God. Allow its meaning to soak into your soul. Then create your own version of this admonition, inserting your own name in the place of the wise man, the strong man, the rich man, the one who boasts, along with some of your own likely subjects of pride. For example: "Let not John Stott boast of his preaching." When you have finished your personalized creation of this declaration, use it as a subject of prayer.

"Let not the wise man boast of his wisdom
   or the strong man boast of his strength
   or the rich man boast of his riches,
but let him who boasts boast about this:
   that he understands and knows me,
   that I am the LORD, who exercises kindness,
     justice and righteousness on earth,
     for in these I delight,"
       declares the LORD. (Jeremiah 9:23-24)

5

Being Led
by the Spirit

1 Corinthians 2:6-16

The Holy Spirit is a restless, inquisitive researcher, somewhat like a deep-sea diver seeking to fathom the depths of the being of God. The Holy Spirit is God exploring the infinity of God. Yet the Holy Spirit also enlightens the minds of God's people to discern what he has revealed to and through biblical authors. In this way he continues his work of illumination into the human sphere. In this section we explore what it means for us his current followers to be led by God's Spirit.

GROUP DISCUSSION. Suppose that you needed information about how to repair a lawn mower. How would you go about getting that knowledge: from a fix-it book, the Internet, a friend? How and why?

PERSONAL REFLECTION. Bring to mind a Christian who you think of as mature and wise in faith. What evidence of spiritual maturity do you see?

This section of Paul's letter places heavy emphasis on the person and ministry of the Holy Spirit. Directly or indirectly he is mentioned up to thirteen times—with a particular focus on his teaching role. *Read 1 Corinthians 2:6-16.*

1. Paul contrasts "the wisdom of this age or of the rulers of this age" with "God's secret wisdom" (vv. 6-7). Where have you seen the "wisdom of this age" displayed recently?

2. When Paul speaks "a message of wisdom among the mature" at Corinth, what are some ways that he describes this wisdom (vv. 6-10)?

3. According to these verses, what role does the Holy Spirit have in making a Christian wise?

4. In verse 9, Paul paraphrases Isaiah 64:4. What thoughts and emotions do these words stir in you? Why?

5. Survey the rest of this passage by titling each of the following segments with a word or phrase about the Holy Spirit:

2:10-11

2:12

2:13

2:14-16

6. Focus again on verses 10-16. This text divides people into two categories: those who operate under the spirit of the world and those who live under the Spirit of God. From these verses, what's true about life under the spirit of the world?

about life under the Spirit of God? (Try to find something in each verse.)

---

7. What risks do you see in living life apart from God's Spirit?

What would you want to say, if you could, to a person you know who seems to be taking the risk of living apart from God's Spirit?

---

8. Scan 1 Corinthians 2:10-16 again. What do you find here to be thankful for in your own experience?

---

9. As you consider your own life under the Spirit of God, what links does God's Spirit create between you and the Word of God?

10. Paul ends this section of his letter with a quote from Isaiah 40:13 where the Old Testament prophet asks, almost without hope, "For who has known the mind of the Lord / that he may instruct him?" Then Paul adds his own astounding statement: "But we have the mind of Christ" (v. 16). What is your emotional and spiritual response to this announcement?

How might it influence your actions?

Consider an area of responsibility in your own leadership where you are most in need of the mind of Christ. Prayerfully draw together all that you know of Christ's being and teachings, and meditate on these. Then ask for his mind to infiltrate your own as you meet this challenge.

Now or Later

This then is the apostolic claim: the same Holy Spirit of God, who searches the depths of God and knows the thoughts of God, and who revealed his findings to the apostles, went on to communicate them to others through the apostles in words that he gave them. He spoke his words through their words, so that their words were simultaneously his. This is the double authorship of Scripture and the meaning of inspiration.

If the above statement is true, then . . . (continue your response in the space below).

6

Moving Toward Maturity

1 Corinthians 3:1-9

We who grow up and grow old in Western culture innately value individualism. Though we become adults, in many ways we are like perpetual two-year-olds shouting, "I want to do it myself!"

The truths of Christianity stand in opposition to this natural culture of ours. God designed us to become something more together than any of us can possibly become alone—his "fellow workers," his "field," his "building."

GROUP DISCUSSION. What are some ways that you enjoy expressing your individuality?

PERSONAL REFLECTION. How do you decide whether to curb the expression of your individuality (or particular expressions of your individuality) and why?

Evangelicals are sometimes criticized for being rugged individualists with a poverty-stricken and even nonexistent theology of the church. If this were true, we would have to depart from the biblical vision, including this chapter; 1 Corinthians 3 is one of the great New Testament chapters on the church. In it, Paul tells the Corinthians bluntly that, in his view, they do not qualify as people who are spiritually mature. As Paul measured it, spiritual maturity has something to do with how Christians balance individual and group identity. *Read 1 Corinthians 3:1-9.*

1. What accusations does Paul make against the Christians of Corinth (vv. 1-4)?

2. How serious a problem do you think jealousy and quarreling are?

Why do you think that?

3. Begin to think more deeply about jealousy and quarreling among Christians. When Christians engage in jealousy and quarreling, what are they saying about themselves?

about God?

about the church?

4. Focus on verses 5-9. Paul opens this section with two questions: "What, after all, is Apollos? And what is Paul?" Use your own words to explain Paul's answer to these questions.

5. Take a few moments of silence to bring to mind one setting where you hope Christians will live out the unity described as "God's fellow workers" or "God's field" or "God's building." (No need to mention any names or settings aloud.) Pray silently for these Christian brothers and sisters.

6. In verses 6-7, Paul summarizes, in the briefest possible manner, all of the events of Acts 18. What does this summary reveal about what it takes to create and sustain a church or Christian ministry?

Where and how have you seen these steps take place?

7. How does Paul's summary in verses 6-7 address the moral failure of Christians who become jealous of one another or who quarrel with each other?

8. Do you think that there are excusable divisions between Christians? If so, give an example.

What are some inexcusable divisions between Christians?

9. How might a Christian leader draw on the principles of this passage to head off unworthy divisions?

---

10. Take stock of some of your own individual strengths or righteous passions. What are some ways that you could channel these strengths or interests into common efforts of your church or ministry?

One of the most encouraging statements of this passage is four words in verse 6: "God made it grow." Pray now, asking God to do this miraculous, mysterious, maturing work in a ministry that is close to your heart.

Now or Later

The Revised English Bible translates verse 9 as, "We are fellow workers [with each other] in God's service." Prayerfully allow God to search your heart as you mentally scan through the names of other Christians with whom you work and serve. Ask him to dig out any hints of jealousy and quarreling that you have allowed to take root. Repent. Determine to find ways that you can blend and bend your own individuality with these people so that you become "God's field" and "God's building" together.

7

Leading in
Ways That Last

1 Corinthians 3:10-23

"I follow Paul." "I follow Apollos." "I follow Cephas." These were the loyalty claims of various Christians in the church of Corinth, claims which Paul felt obligated to thoroughly debunk. Yet the question of who we are following in the church remains a vital issue. Today some may follow a particular worship leader because they like their style of music best. Others might follow a certain pastor whose sermons make them feel good. Still others may regard as truth only the words of the person who led them to Christ in the first place.

We urgently need a healthy, biblical understanding of the church, for only then shall we have a healthy, biblical understanding of Christian leadership.

GROUP DISCUSSION. If you were asked to give one sentence of advice to a new leader in your church, what would you say? Begin your answer with the word *always* or *never*.

PERSONAL REFLECTION. If a person were to say, "I follow _____ (insert your name)," what do you hope that person would mean—and not mean?

Paul uses two images to help the Corinthian Christians better understand the nature of God's church: a building under construction, and then a particular kind of building—a temple. *Read 1 Corinthians 3:10-23.*

1. If you were one of the leaders in the church of Corinth, how would you feel as you heard this section of Paul's letter: encouraged, discouraged, worried or challenged? Why?

2. Focus on verses 10-15 where Paul pictures the church as a building under construction. What do various terms in the passage represent: expert builder, foundation, various building materials, revealed, fire, the Day?

3. What role does "fire" have in the development of a church?

What people or events have served as "fire" in your own experience?

4. What does the "one foundation" statement of verse 11 imply about the nature of a true church?

5. In a church, almost everyone teaches something to someone, even if unintentionally. When you consider those within your own influence as a teacher, what cautions and what hopes especially jump out as you think about Paul's illustration of a church as a building under construction?

6. Read verses 16-17 again. Mentally run your eyes up and down the rows of people who typically gather at your church for worship. How can you relate to these people in a way that shows that together (not individually) you become something as holy and as beautiful as God's temple? (Consider those you relate easily to, as well as those who are not so easy to relate to.)

7. This passage also carries the warning of verse 17. What are some of the destructive forces in your church that might come under that warning?

8. What responsibility can you take to protect your church from these kinds of destructive forces?

9. Read verses 18-21 again. What chain of belonging can you find?

10. In your own church setting how can you show appropriate respect for your leaders—but not fall into the sin of boasting about them? Give examples of both—showing respect and boasting—to distinguish between the two.

11. "So then, no more boasting about men!" (1 Corinthians 3:21). And, "Let him who boasts boast in the Lord" (1 Corinthians 1:31). If you were to seriously enact these two statements about boasting as you relate to people within your own cluster of Christian friends, what changes would begin to take place?

Pray, thanking God for people within your church who have helped you to feel that this gathering of varied people is "God's temple." Ask his blessing on them, on their continued service within that body of people—and to the world beyond. Pray too that he will give you humility and wisdom as you lead.

Now or Later

Check the "foundation" of your building under construction. At the next gathering of your church, look for evidence that Jesus Christ is the foundation. Notice Scripture passages, phrases in songs, words of testimony, coffee table conversations, creeds, artistic symbols, banners, prayers, sermons, sacraments, class notes. Create a list of all references to Jesus and evaluate the evidence of Christ's position in your church. Foundation? Peripheral? Barely evident? Consider your part in strengthening or affirming Christ as the foundation of your church.

Read and meditate on the hymn "The Church's One Foundation" by Samuel J. Stone.

8

Keeping a Clear Conscience

1 Corinthians 4:1-7

There is much contemporary confusion about the nature of the ordained pastoral ministry. What are clergy? Are they primarily priests, presbyters, pastors, prophets, preachers or psychotherapists? Are they administrators, facilitators, managers, social workers, evangelists or liturgists? The uncertainty is not new. Throughout its long and checkered history, the church has oscillated between the opposite extremes of clericalism (which puts clergy on a pedestal) and anticlericalism (which knocks them off again). Now that many churches have recovered the Pauline vision of the "every-member-ministry" of the body of Christ, radical questions are being asked once again. Are clergy necessary any longer? Are they not superfluous? Wouldn't the church be healthier without them? Actually, this confusion goes right back to the beginning. The first-century Corinthian church divided into different factions that were each claiming the patronage of particular teachers: "I belong to Paul . . . Apollos . . . Peter." Paul was horrified by this personality cult. "*What* on earth do you think we are?" he asks.

GROUP DISCUSSION. What do you think is hard about being a leader in Christian settings?

PERSONAL REFLECTION. What triggers temptation to pride in your own settings of leadership—and how do you cope with that temptation?

Paul's illumination here of the character and role those in leadership are to have encourages us to lead with integrity in the midst of the pressure leadership brings. *Read 1 Corinthians 4:1-7.*

1. In view of this reading, draw a leadership chart showing Paul, the Corinthian Christians and God. Don't forget to include in your chart's structure Paul's statement to the Corinthians, "All things are yours, whether Paul or Apollos or Cephas" (3:21).

2. Where would you put yourself on that chart—as you relate to other Christians and as you relate to God?

What responsibilities and cautions does your spot include?

3. Paul says that Christian leaders have one responsibility; they "must prove faithful" to God (v. 2). What did that mean to Paul?

What does it mean to you?

4. Paul tells the Corinthians in verse 5 to "judge nothing" and says that he does not even judge himself. Yet chapters 5—8 are full of his instructive judgment on the church at Corinth. (He also wrote to them the beautiful love chapter of 1 Corinthians 13.) How do you think Paul would explain the judging portion of his letter in view of his command to the Corinthians not to judge him?

5. All leaders receive criticism—sometimes cruelly. How can 1 Corinthians 4:1-7 help you respond to criticism?

6. Often leaders carry a public face that brushes away hurtful personal attacks, but the hurt remains. What do you find here that might heal some of those hurts?

7. Consider more carefully Paul's words, "My conscience is clear, but that does not make me innocent" (v. 4). What are some practices that will help a Christian leader keep a clear conscience?

8. Notice the three questions of verse 7. How would the answers to these questions affect the way a Christian leader relates to people under his or her influence?

9. The sins of pride and boasting tempt all leaders. Some grow adept at subtle ways to inform others of their successes without appearing to boast. If you were tempted to pride and boasting, what would you find in these seven verses that might help you resist those sins?

10. As you reflect on this passage, are you more or less willing to accept leadership roles? Why?

Pray for a Christian leader currently under fire.

Now or Later

Prayerfully examine yourself for any hint of pride in your own leadership. Then read Romans 12:1-21 aloud as God's instructions to you.

9

Cultivating a Gentle Spirit

1 Corinthians 4:8-21

James Stalker was a Scottish minister and author at the end of the nineteenth century. In one of his books he wrote:

> When I first was settled in a church, I discovered a thing of which nobody had told me, and which I had not anticipated, but which proved a tremendous aid in doing the work of the ministry. I fell in love with my congregation. I do not know how otherwise to express it. It was as genuine a blossom of the heart as any which I have ever experienced. It made it easy to do anything for my people.[*]

We can only imagine the powerful spiritual nurture that came from a pastor who had fallen in love with his people.

GROUP DISCUSSION. We have all had many leaders: parents, scout leaders, bosses at work, teachers, pastors, youth workers, committee chairs and many others. Name one person who you have valued as a leader. Why?

PERSONAL REFLECTION. When and why do you enjoy leading? (Be as

---

[*] James Stalker, *The Preacher and His Models* (London: Hodder & Stoughton, 1891), p. 231.

honest with yourself as you are able.) What hints of pride and power do you find in these motives?

In 1 Corinthians 4, the apostle Paul uses several vivid metaphors from the Greco-Roman world to illustrate true Christian leadership—leadership that acts out of love and gentleness for those being led. *Read 1 Corinthians 4:8-21.*

1. As you view the content of the three major sections of this text, what voice tones do you detect by the content of each (vv. 8-13, 14-17, 18-21)? Try reading this text aloud using these voice inflections.

2. What vivid pictures do you see in Paul's descriptions of the apostolic leaders, including himself (vv. 8-13)?

3. What principles of Christian leadership can you gather from these same verses?

4. Paul seems to think that the Corinthians have enjoyed their many opportunities for wealth and education and freedom to practice any form of religion, but somehow they've became spiritually poor and immature in the process. Most people in today's Western culture have similar opportunities—and temptations. What caution can you personally take from Paul's contrast of apostolic leadership and Corinthian leadership?

5. How does Paul's picture of children in a wealthy family help illustrate what his relationship is and is not to the Corinthians (vv. 14-17)?

_____

6. What can you know from these verses about Paul's ministry in Christian churches beyond Corinth?

_____

7. "I urge you to imitate me," says Paul in verse 16. When have you said (or heard) similar words as a parent or from a parent?

_____

8. What would it take for you to be able to say these words with some degree of integrity as a spiritual leader?

_____

9. Paul promises (threatens?) a personal visit in verses 18-21. He asks the Corinthians to choose whether he is to come with a whip or "in love and with a gentle spirit." His letter demonstrates that he is capable of both. If you were a leader in the Corinthian church, how would you help your church prepare for Paul's arrival?

10. "Love and . . . a gentle spirit" is not a common description of leaders. When and how have you seen it expressed in a Christian leader?

Pray that Christian leaders may be characterized above all else by what the apostle Paul called "the meekness and gentleness of Christ" (2 Corinthians 10:1).

Now or Later

In prayer, name before God several Christian leaders whom you know or know of. Pray for the unique situations each faces. Ask God to grant the strength of gentleness wherever needed.

Leader's Notes

MY GRACE IS SUFFICIENT FOR YOU. (2 COR 12:9)

Leading a Bible discussion can be an enjoyable and rewarding experience. But it can also be scary especially if you've never done it before. If this is your feeling, you're in good company. When God asked Moses to lead the Israelites out of Egypt, he replied, "O Lord, please send someone else to do it!" (Ex 4:13). It was the same with Solomon, Jeremiah and Timothy, but God helped these people in spite of their weaknesses, and he will help you as well.

You don't need to be an expert on the Bible or a trained teacher to lead a Bible discussion. The idea behind these inductive studies is that the leader guides group members to discover for themselves what the Bible has to say. This method of learning will allow group members to remember much more of what is said than a lecture would.

These studies are designed to be led easily. As a matter of fact, the flow of questions through the passage from observation to interpretation to application is so natural that you may feel that the studies lead themselves. This study guide is also flexible. You can use it with a variety of groups student, professional, neighborhood or church groups. Each study takes forty-five to sixty minutes in a group setting.

There are some important facts to know about group dynamics and encouraging discussion. The suggestions listed below should enable you to effectively and enjoyably fulfill your role as leader.

Preparing for the Study

1. Ask God to help you understand and apply the passage in your own life. Unless this happens, you will not be prepared to lead others. Pray too for the various members of the group. Ask God to open your hearts to the message of his Word and motivate you to action.

2. Read the introduction to the entire guide to get an overview of the entire book and the issues which will be explored.

3. As you begin each study, read and reread the assigned Bible passage to familiarize yourself with it.

4. This study guide is based on the New International Version of the Bible. It will help you and the group if you use this translation as the basis for your study and discussion.

5. Carefully work through each question in the study. Spend time in meditation and reflection as you consider how to respond.

6. Write your thoughts and responses in the space provided in the study guide. This will help you to express your understanding of the passage clearly.

7. It might help to have a Bible dictionary handy. Use it to look up any unfamiliar words, names or places. (For additional help on how to study a passage, see chapter five of *How to Lead a LifeGuide Bible Study,* InterVarsity Press.)

8. Consider how you can apply the Scripture to your life. Remember that the group will follow your lead in responding to the studies. They will not go any deeper than you do.

9. Once you have finished your own study of the passage, familiarize yourself with the leader's notes for the study you are leading. These are designed to help you in several ways. First, they tell you the purpose the study guide author had in mind when writing the study. Take time to think through how the study questions work together to accomplish that purpose. Second, the notes provide you with additional background information or suggestions on group dynamics for various questions. This information can be useful when people have difficulty understanding or answering a question. Third, the leader's notes can alert you to potential problems you may encounter during the study.

10. If you wish to remind yourself of anything mentioned in the leader's notes, make a note to yourself below that question in the study.

Leading the Study

1. Begin the study on time. Open with prayer, asking God to help the group to understand and apply the passage.

2. Be sure that everyone in your group has a study guide. Encourage the group to prepare beforehand for each discussion by reading the introduction to the guide and by working through the questions in the study.

3. At the beginning of your first time together, explain that these studies are meant to be discussions, not lectures. Encourage the members of the group to participate. However, do not put pressure on those who may be hesitant to speak during the first few sessions. You may want to suggest the following guidelines to your group.

☐ Stick to the topic being discussed.

☐ Your responses should be based on the verses which are the focus of the discussion and not on outside authorities such as commentaries or speakers.

☐ These studies focus on a particular passage of Scripture. Only rarely should you refer to other portions of the Bible. This allows for everyone to participate in in-depth study on equal ground.

☐ Anything said in the group is considered confidential and will not be discussed outside the group unless specific permission is given to do so.

☐ We will listen attentively to each other and provide time for each person present to talk.

☐ We will pray for each other.

4. Have a group member read the introduction at the beginning of the discussion.

5. Every session begins with a group discussion question. The question or activity is meant to be used before the passage is read. The question introduces the theme of the study and encourages group members to begin to open up. Encourage as many members as possible to participate, and be ready to get the discussion going with your own response.

This section is designed to reveal where our thoughts or feelings need to be transformed by Scripture. That is why it is especially important not to read the passage before the discussion question is asked. The passage will tend to color the honest reactions people would otherwise give because they are, of course, supposed to think the way the Bible does.

You may want to supplement the group discussion question with an icebreaker to help people to get comfortable. See the community section of *Small Group Idea Book* for more ideas.

You also might want to use the personal reflection question with your group. Either allow a time of silence for people to respond individually or discuss it together.

6. Have a group member (or members if the passage is long) read aloud the passage to be studied. Then give people several minutes to read the passage again silently so that they can take it all in.

7. Question 1 will generally be an overview question designed to briefly survey the passage. Encourage the group to look at the whole passage, but try to avoid getting sidetracked by questions or issues that will be addressed later in the study.

8. As you ask the questions, keep in mind that they are designed to be used just as they are written. You may simply read them aloud. Or you may prefer to express them in your own words.

There may be times when it is appropriate to deviate from the study guide. For example, a question may have already been answered. If so, move on to the next question. Or someone may raise an important question not covered in the guide. Take time to discuss it, but try to keep the group from going off on tangents.

9. Avoid answering your own questions. If necessary, repeat or rephrase

them until they are clearly understood. Or point out something you read in the leader's notes to clarify the context or meaning. An eager group quickly becomes passive and silent if they think the leader will do most of the talking.

10. Don't be afraid of silence. People may need time to think about the question before formulating their answers.

11. Don't be content with just one answer. Ask, "What do the rest of you think?" or "Anything else?" until several people have given answers to the question.

12. Acknowledge all contributions. Try to be affirming whenever possible. Never reject an answer. If it is clearly off-base, ask, "Which verse led you to that conclusion?" or again, "What do the rest of you think?"

13. Don't expect every answer to be addressed to you, even though this will probably happen at first. As group members become more at ease, they will begin to truly interact with each other. This is one sign of healthy discussion.

14. Don't be afraid of controversy. It can be very stimulating. If you don't resolve an issue completely, don't be frustrated. Move on and keep it in mind for later. A subsequent study may solve the problem.

15. Periodically summarize what the group has said about the passage. This helps to draw together the various ideas mentioned and gives continuity to the study. But don't preach.

16. At the end of the Bible discussion you may want to allow group members a time of quiet to work on an idea under "Now or Later." Then discuss what you experienced. Or you may want to encourage group members to work on these ideas between meetings. Give an opportunity during the session for people to talk about what they are learning.

17. Conclude your time together with conversational prayer, adapting the prayer suggestion at the end of the study to your group. Ask for God's help in following through on the commitments you've made.

18. End on time.

Many more suggestions and helps are found in *How to Lead a LifeGuide Bible Study.*

Components of Small Groups

A healthy small group should do more than study the Bible. There are four components to consider as you structure your time together.

Nurture. Small groups help us to grow in our knowledge and love of God. Bible study is the key to making this happen and is the foundation of your small group.

Community. Small groups are a great place to develop deep friendships with other Christians. Allow time for informal interaction before and after each study. Plan activities and games that will help you get to know each other. Spend time having fun together going on a picnic or cooking dinner together.

Worship and prayer. Your study will be enhanced by spending time praising God together in prayer or song. Pray for each other's needs and keep track of how God is answering prayer in your group. Ask God to help you to apply what you are learning in your study.

Outreach. Reaching out to others can be a practical way of applying what you are learning, and it will keep your group from becoming self-focused. Host a series of evangelistic discussions for your friends or neighbors. Clean up the yard of an elderly friend. Serve at a soup kitchen together, or spend a day working on a Habitat house.

Many more suggestions and helps in each of these areas are found in *Small Group Idea Book*. Information on building a small group can be found in *Small Group Leaders' Handbook* and *The Big Book on Small Groups* (both from InterVarsity Press). Reading through one of these books would be worth your time.

Study 1. Seeing Gifting in God's Imperfect People. 1 Corinthians 1:1-9.

Purpose: To be encouraged by God's work among imperfect people in our imperfect churches.

General note. Since the book of 1 Corinthians was written to a church and mostly deals with church matters, many questions in this study guide assume that readers are part of a church. If this is not true in your particular group, you will need to rephrase several questions so that people respond in a "what if" manner: "If I were in a church I would expect, hope, plan, think, etc." Even though the church at Corinth received this strong (but loving) letter of admonition, it also served as an encouragement to the nonchurched that life within the church is God's expected norm for all of his people. The church is one of the ways he grows us into all that he has designed us to be.

Question 3. Look for words of connection: "together," "our(s)," "with." Notice who is connected to whom in almost every verse of the text. If you're wondering who Sosthenes was, Leon Morris writes in *1 Corinthians* that this "may be the Jewish 'synagogue ruler' (Acts 18:17), in which case he was subsequently converted. But the name is not uncommon and it may not be the same man" (Tyndale New Testament Commentary [Downers Grove, Ill.: InterVarsity Press, 1985; reprint, Downers Grove, Ill.: IVP Academic, 2008], p. 35 [page citations are to the original edition]).

Question 5. The term "day of our Lord" in the Old Testament often referred to the day or time of God's judgment. Here, the apostle Paul adds the name Jesus Christ to this saying, a name that he uses nine times in as many verses. Paul also adds the familial term *our* to Lord Jesus Christ. Morris writes, "Here the thought [about this day] is that because it is [our Lord's] day and because it is he who will 'guarantee' the Corinthians, they may be assured that they will be *blameless* in that day. No charge can be laid against those whom Christ guarantees (*cf.* Rom. 8:33)" (Leon Morris, *1 Corinthians*, p. 38).

Question 10. Encourage several people in your group to express personal reflections on this question. If they need some prompting, you can read them the following: Even though the Corinthian church had been wonderfully graced and enriched in every way in Christ so that it lacked nothing, it was still not blameless. That is why they were still *eagerly waiting for our Lord Jesus Christ to be revealed* (v. 7). Not only would he keep them *strong to the end,* but in consequence they *would be blameless* on that day (v. 8). Enriched now, we shall be blameless then. We know this not because of our faith, but because of God's faithfulness. Having called us into fellowship with Christ, into our common participation in Christ, he will one day perfect our participation in him. "God called us" is a past reality; "fellowship with Christ" is the present experience; "God is faithful" is the ground of our confidence for the future.

Study 2. Bringing Unity in the Midst of Division. 1 Corinthians 1:10-17.

Purpose: To follow Paul's teachings to the Corinthians and thereby bring healing to fractured relationships in our own churches and Christian groups.

General note. The opening section of 1 Corinthians obliges us to reflect on the ambiguity of the church and to come to terms with it. On the one hand, biblical Christians are not perfectionists who dream of developing a perfect church on earth. On the other hand, biblical Christians are not defeatists who tolerate all manner of sin and error in the church.

To perfectionists we say, "You are right to seek the purity of the church. The doctrinal and ethical purity of the church is a proper goal of Christian endeavor. But you are wrong to imagine that you will attain it. Not until Christ comes will he present his bride to himself as 'a radiant church, without stain or wrinkle or any other blemish, but holy and blameless'" (Eph 5:27).

To defeatists we say, "You are right to acknowledge the reality of sin and error in the church, and not to close your eyes to it. But you are wrong to tolerate it. There is a place for discipline in the church, and even for excommunication. To deny the divine-human person of Jesus Christ is antichrist (1 Jn 2:22). To deny the gospel of grace is to deserve God's anathema (Gal 1:6-9). We cannot condone these things."

In these days we are living in the painful tension between the already and the not yet. Only when Christ comes will the ideal become reality, and all ambiguity cease.

As you guide the discussion of 1 Corinthians 1:10-17, bear in mind the ambiguity in which we live. We (and our churches) *already* belong to Christ; but we are *not yet* made perfect. You may find it helpful to draw on the reflections above to guide your response to the biblical text—and to the warring parties of your own Christian environment.

Question 2. Notice several words that point toward unity: "brothers," "our," "all," "agree," "no divisions," "united." These words point toward unity, but they also state purpose and method. Notice that, while other names appear throughout the passage, here we read only "our Lord Jesus Christ."

Question 3. Jesus himself rooted words and actions in the mind and the heart. We speak and act because of what we silently cherish inside ourselves. (See Mt 12:34-35 and Mk 7:14-15, along with events of their context.) If we participate in division among Christ-followers, the root of that division likely sprouts from the self-centered brooding that we allow our hearts and minds.

Question 6. Help your group trace the flow of Paul's argument and figure out his major emphasis. His emphasis is on Christ and the unity of his people because they are united under and in and through Christ. Baptism may have been a divisive point in this church, in that one who baptized converts might have then been their assumed leader. It would take much humility from a Christian leader to notice this misplacement of confidence—as Paul does—and redirect it toward Christ.

Question 7. Conflict is inevitable among flawed (though redeemed) humans, and conflict almost invariably causes us to focus on people who may disagree about honestly held and important issues. But rather than divide the church, we must face and then resolve these conflicts—exercising forgiveness when needed—and move on to our main purpose. Christ was crucified for our salvation, and he rose so that we can spend eternity with him. God commissions us to share this gift. Time and energy absorbed by internal bickering will almost certainly decrease our ability, at least for a time, to be about our primary purpose to worship God and point others to him. Additionally, people rarely feel drawn to a warring church, or other Christian group, and so (for them) the magnet of the cross is "emptied of its power."

Question 10. If you are using this study in a group setting, allow several minutes of silent soul-searching so that people may use the first two questions to examine their motives in the presence of this biblical admonition. Then discuss responses to the final question of this set.

Study 3. Finding Power in Weakness. 1 Corinthians 1:18-25.

Purpose: To understand and take hold of the power of the cross and to follow Jesus' example of a self-sacrificing use of power.

Question 1. This passage is full of contextual oddities: the perishing and the saved (v. 18), a cross with power (v. 18), wisdom destroyed—by God (v. 19), intelligence frustrated (v. 19), wisdom made foolish (v. 20), foolish preaching (v. 21), Christ a stumbling block (v. 23), foolishness of God (v. 25), weakness of God (v. 25). Even without fully understanding how all of this fits together from God's perspective, we can see at a glance that God's view of power, wisdom, foolishness and crucifixion do not fit into ordinary relationship with each other.

Question 2. This is a fairly complex section of Paul's letter, partly because of the various unlikely matches of words and concepts, and partly because of the convoluted sentence structure. It also raises a number of questions about meaning and implications: Why would God destroy wisdom? Is good preaching foolish? Is this passage supporting intentional ignorance? Let your group express these or other questions, then use your continued discussion of the text to explore possible answers. As part of the discussion leader's preparation, work through the exercise in the "Now or Later" section. This will reveal some of the connections, opposites and pairs of the text—and therefore help resolve some of the questions.

As an additional note, verse 19 is a quotation from Isaiah 29:14, immediately followed by the famous illustration of the potter and the clay where the clay rises up and declares of the potter: "He did not make me. He knows nothing." It is to this kind of rebellious "clay" that God says, through the apostle Paul, that he will destroy their wisdom and frustrate their intelligence, for they have not recognized their potter and have tried to put themselves in his place. Paul wants the Corinthians (and us) to know that a failure to recognize Jesus as God, and his crucifixion as the power of salvation for all who believe, is like clay spouting off clay-bound wisdom to its potter.

Question 4. In the beautifully chiseled sentence of verse 21, we find that human beings cannot reach God by themselves. God is infinite, we are finite. God is holy, we are sinners. In consequence, we are doubly cut off from God. So God has taken the initiative to do what we cannot do, namely, bridge the gulf between us. Verse 21 contains three contrasts, which emerge as three questions. By answering them you will discern much of the mystery of this text: Who took the initiative to reach us? What was the result of God's initiative? How was the initiative taken?

Question 6. It is interesting to notice that though Jews were looking for "miraculous signs" (and "Christ crucified" became their "stumbling block," a stone they tripped over), and Greeks were looking for "wisdom" (and they considered the preaching of Christ crucified as "foolishness"), still God called some from each group. And for these called ones among both Jews and Greeks, "the message of the cross" became the "power of God." Use this question to put yourself into the sandals of that New Testament gospel-bearer. How would you present "the message of the cross" to those who looked for a powerful Messiah?

Question 7. The power of the cross was in Christ's utter abandonment of self-interest on behalf of those who would believe and accept his sacrifice— for them. People who model that kind of power think of the needs of those they're serving and then make purposeful decisions out of love, based on those needs.

Question 9. The cross is the power of God, because through it God saves those who cannot save themselves. It is also the wisdom of God, because through it God has solved not only *our* problem (sin and guilt) but *his own*. It is not wrong to speak of a divine problem or dilemma solved at the cross. This problem arose from God's character of holy love. How could he express his holiness in punishing evil without compromising his love? How could he express his love in forgiving sinners without compromising his justice? How could he be at one and the same time "a righteous God and a Savior" (Is 45:21)? His answer to these questions was and still is the cross. For on the cross he took our place, bore our sin, died our death, and so paid our debt.

Question 10. We all deal with temptations to misuse our power, whether it is while leading a nation or potty-training a toddler. Encourage your group members to consider the sacrifice of the cross as their own model for abandoning a selfish use of power. Power feeds our desire to get our way, manipulate people, make ourselves look good. However, the power of the cross was not brute force but love. In our own power-settings, we too need to express love, grace and sacrifice for others, as did our model Jesus Christ. Use this question to guide people into specific ways to live out these principles in their own settings.

Study 4. Placing Confidence in Christ. 1 Corinthians 1:26—2:5.

Purpose: To discover that our true strength is in Christ, not self.

Question 1. Discuss phrases as well as concepts throughout the passage.

Question 2. Notice the repeated phrase "not many." It is evident from these verses that most of the Corinthian converts were drawn from the lower ranks of society. Mostly they did not belong to the intelligentsia, or to the city's influential leaders, or to its aristocracy. On the whole they would have been regarded as uneducated, insignificant, poor and socially despised, being probably slaves (see also 1 Cor 7:21). But this was not the only population of the Corinthian church.

Saul of Tarsus, with his brilliant intellect, was himself an exception to his own rule. Luke tells us that Crispus (the ruler of the synagogue in Corinth) was converted (Acts 18:8). And in Romans 16:23-24 (a letter written from Corinth) Paul sent greetings from both Gaius (wealthy enough to give hospitality to the whole church) and Erastus (described as "the city's director of public works"). Moreover, both 1 and 2 Corinthians imply that some Corinthian Christians were well-to-do (see 1 Cor 11:22; 16:2, 15, 19; 2 Cor 8—9). For the church in Corinth, like for Christian churches throughout the centuries, the shared faith of true believers crossed all other lines of separation, bringing a healthy blend of people from all segments of society.

Today, though, the common thought remains in some Christian circles that God prefers those who are physically, educationally or emotionally deprived, and therefore we ought not to explore higher learning for ourselves if we want to truly know God. This is an erroneous conclusion. A spiritually mature church does not reject the poor or the rich, the uneducated or the educated, if they are followers of Christ.

Paul's emphasis in this text is that God's power operates only in the salvation of "the weak." Therefore, if "the strong" hope to be saved, they must acknowledge their weakness (their inability to save themselves). Otherwise the grace of God cannot reach them. As Jesus put it, the kingdom of God belongs only to children. If, therefore, adults want to enter it, they have to become like children themselves (Mk 10:13-16). Luther understood this well.

> Only the prisoner shall be free;
> Only the poor shall be rich;
> Only the weak shall be strong;
> Only the humble exalted;
> Only the empty filled;
> Only nothing shall be something.

Question 3. Verse 30 is a complex verse with many nuances about who Jesus is and what he accomplished and continues to accomplish. Encourage your group to work with various words and phrases in this verse as they bring out these pictures of Jesus. After the discussion, the following observations may be helpful: The credit for their salvation belonged to God alone. It is *because of him* (God) *that you are in Christ Jesus.* God the Father had united them to Christ, so (Paul now associates himself with the Corinthians) Christ *has become for us,* on the one hand, *wisdom from God* and, on the other hand, *our righteousness, holiness and redemption* (v. 30). These three great blessings we enjoy in Christ are surely the three tenses of salvation: past (our justification), present (our sanctification) and future (our glorification, including the redemption of our bodies).

Question 6. See 1 Corinthians 1:29 and 2:5.

Question 7. Allow people in your group to speculate about how Paul might be received in their own churches—especially as he describes himself in this text. Don't forget to note "the Spirit's power" of verse 2:4. Afterward, if it seems of interest, you might add that Paul may have been contrasting his own presentation of the gospel with the kind of rhetoric popular in Corinthian culture of that day. Rhetoric was a systematic, academic discipline taught and practiced throughout the Greco-Roman world. In fact, in the first century A.D., rhetoric became the primary discipline in Roman higher education. In public debates, in the law courts and at funerals the rhetoric of display and ornamentation was tremendously popular as a form of public entertainment. Gradually it became an end in itself, mere ornamentation, with a desire to please the crowd—without serious content or intent. A sophist was an orator who emphasized style over substance, form over content. The goal was applause, the motive vanity and the casualty truth.

Study 5. Being Led by the Spirit. 1 Corinthians 2:6-16.

Purpose: To understand the Holy Spirit's role in guiding us and growing our discernment, that we might lead wisely.

Question 2. Encourage your group to look for insights about true wisdom in almost every phrase of verses 6-10. Among other things they should note that wisdom is "among the mature" (v. 6), that wisdom is from God (v. 7), that God destined this wisdom "for our glory" (v. 7). Other references to wisdom throughout Paul's letters to the Corinthians will further amplify this gift of wisdom, which includes not only regeneration and justification, but also resurrection of the body and renewal of the universe.

Question 3. Paul insists in verse 9 that all human beings, if left to themselves, are ignorant of God's will and purpose. God's wisdom is something "no eye has seen" (it is invisible), "no ear has heard" (it is inaudible) and "no mind has conceived" (it is inconceivable). It is altogether beyond the reach of human eyes, ears and minds. It cannot be grasped either by scientific investigation or by poetic imagination. It is absolutely unattainable by our little, finite, fallen and fallible minds. It can be known only if God should choose to make it known—which is exactly what he has done: "God has revealed it to us by his Spirit" (v. 10).

Question 5. One biblical analyst titled these sections "The Searching Spirit" (2:10-11), "The Revealing Spirit" (2:10, 12), "The Inspiring Spirit" (2:13) and "The Enlightening Spirit" (2:13-16). Your group may come up with similar insights or some variation of them.

Question 7. Consider descriptions of this kind of person as given in verses 11 and 14. Consider also that life under "the spirit of the world" would mean an absence of those gifts promised here particularly to those who live under the Spirit of God.

Study 6. Moving Toward Maturity. 1 Corinthians 3:1-9.

Purpose: To identify and admit the sins of jealousy and quarreling between Christians and to move on toward spiritual maturity.

Question 1. You should find between eight and ten descriptive words and phrases in these four verses.

Question 3. This is a complex question that will come up throughout the study. At this point, try to highlight preliminary answers in all three areas, but expect to expand on these insights as the study progresses.

Question 4. Paul replied to his own questions as to who he and Apollos were: "only servants, through whom you came to believe" (v. 5). That is, Paul and Apollos were not masters to whom the Corinthians owed allegiance but servants—only servants. Moreover, they were not servants *in* whom the Corinthians had believed, for they were not the objects of their faith. Neither were they servants *from* whom the Corinthians had believed, for they were not the authors of their faith. But they were servants *through* whom the Corinthians had come to believe (agents or instruments through whom God had worked to elicit their faith). Further, this came about *as the Lord has assigned to each his task*. All parts of verse 5 are designed to demote, even debunk, the leaders whom the Corinthians were improperly elevating.

- These leaders were only things (in the neuter), instruments of divine activity.

- They were only servants, agents through whom God had worked.

- They were only doing the job that had been assigned to them by the Lord.

So neither the Corinthians nor their leaders have anything to boast about.

Question 6. There are three main tasks to be done if a field is to produce a harvest, namely planting the seed, watering the seed and causing the seed to sprout; or sowing, irrigating and growing. Paul applied this to Corinth historically or chronologically in verse 6.

- First, *I planted the seed*. That is, Paul reached Corinth first, during his second missionary journey, and evangelized the city (see Acts 18:1-18).

- Next, *Apollos watered it*. He followed Paul to Corinth (Acts 18:27-28). These two men accomplished their pioneer tasks in relation to the seed.

- But *God made it grow*.

Question 7. In verse 7 Paul compares with one another the three actors—namely himself, Apollos and God—involved in the evangelization of Corinth and the establishment of its church. "So neither he who plants nor he who waters is anything." Both planting and watering are unskilled and somewhat mechanical jobs. Anybody can do them. It requires no professional expertise to drop seeds into soil or to sprinkle water on the seeds sown. A Ph.D. is not necessary. No, what really counts and is indispensable is the mysterious third stage, which causes the seed to sprout and bear fruit. No human being can do this. Paul could not do it with all his apostolic authority. Apollos could not do it with all his knowledge of Scripture and his famous eloquence. *It is only God who makes things grow.*

Question 8. In a group setting, this question might degrade into the sin of gossip. As a leader, do not permit this digression. If discussion of real current divisions is potentially harmful, ask your group to omit all names or give imaginary examples of worthy or unworthy divisions. Some would say

that the Protestant/Catholic division of the sixteenth century was a worthy
division that resulted in necessary correction for both sides. (Some will disagree.) Others may cite some of today's divisions about worship style and
music choices as "unworthy" divisions. Others will likely disagree with this
as well. Nevertheless, the subject of worthy and unworthy division can itself
become a "worthy" discussion, as people consider their own responsibilities
in Christian leadership.

Study 7. Leading in Ways That Last. 1 Corinthians 3:10-23.
Purpose: To build lasting unity into the community of believers to which we
belong.
Question 2. If it is not already obvious to your group, be sure that everyone
understands that Paul is speaking of the local body of believers gathered—
not the church building. In the first century a designated church building
would have been foreign to most Christians; their church met in one another's homes.
Question 3. In many other places in Scripture, fire is a purifier; it purges
away what is untrue or unworthy. Here, however, the image of fire is that of
a revealer. The fire reveals what is durable and what is not. The fire that Paul
describes here will reveal inadequate teachers with wrong or weak teachings
or who do not live out their beliefs and teachings. What will be the result
of this trial by fire? Just as there are two possible materials, so there will be
two results. On the one hand, if the builder's work is made of durable mate-
rial (gold, silver, marble) it will survive, and "he will receive his reward" (v.
14). On the other hand, if his work is made of combustible materials (wood,
hay, straw), it will be consumed. In this case "he will suffer loss," and his
teaching will be seen to be valueless. But in the mercy of God "he himself
will be saved, but only as one escaping through the flames" (v. 15). The
builder's God-given role in the church will be thoroughly discredited by
his own activities. He will lose the reward of seeing his work prosper in the
church—but he won't lose his salvation. The purpose of this fire is not to
purify, but to test and judge.
Question 4. Builders should not tamper with a house's foundation once it
has been laid, trying to dig it up or relay it. "For no one can lay any foundation other than the one already laid, which is Jesus Christ" (v. 11). This is
the foundation Paul had laid (v. 10). As we love to sing, "The church's one
foundation is Jesus Christ her Lord," and this is the Jesus of the apostolic
witness, who is the only authentic Jesus—namely, Jesus the crucified one.
"Paul does not mean," writes C. K. Barrett, "that it would be impossible to
construct a community on a different basis, only that such a community
would not be the church" (*The First Epistle to the Corinthians,* Black's New
Testament Commentaries, 2nd ed. [London: A. & C. Black, 1971], p. 87).

Question 5. Guide people in your group to interact personally with this question as they consider their own settings and their own leadership. Specific names, roles and situations might not be appropriate as you guide your group to reflect on Paul's challenge. Paul issues a solemn warning here to all Christian teachers. The Christian teaching ministry is of the greatest importance because it is designed to build up the church. If what we teach is true, biblical and balanced, we will be adding a valuable building to the foundation, and it will last. If, however, our teaching is unbiblical—the wisdom of the world—then we are adding a ramshackle superstructure that will not survive. Thus what we are teaching will bless or harm the church, not only for this life but even for eternity.

Question 6. Be as specific regarding actions and feelings as is appropriate for your group. The following background may provide perspective for Paul's transition from a literal temple to a "temple" composed of a huge variety of people. In the Old Testament, the essence of the temple in Jerusalem, as was true of the tabernacle before it, was that it was the dwelling place of God. "I will dwell among them," God had said (Ex 25:8). He promised that the Shekinah glory, the visible symbol of his presence, would inhabit and illumine the holy of holies. And the major promise regarding the rebuilt temple was that "the name of the city . . . will be THE LORD IS THERE" (Ezek 48:35). In the New Testament, however, God's temple or dwelling place is his people. Now the individual Christian's body (1 Cor 6:19), now the local church (1 Cor 3:16) and now the universal church (including Gentiles) "are being built together to become a dwelling in which God lives by his Spirit" (Eph 2:22). So in God's sanctuary today—namely, the church—there is neither an image (as in pagan temples) or a symbol (like the Shekinah glory in the Jerusalem temple) but the Holy Spirit of God himself (1 Cor 3:16).

The sacred wonder of the church, therefore, is that it is the dwelling place of God by his Spirit. Of course, "church" means people, not buildings, and God's presence is tied not to buildings but to his covenant people, to whom he has pledged himself. Wherever they are, there he is also—especially when they assemble for worship, even in small numbers, for then he is there in their midst (Mt 18:20). He promises also to be with them as they go about their various missions to the world (Mt 28:20).

Question 7. Because of the sacred nature of the Christian community as the dwelling place of God, it must not be dishonored in any way—divided by jealousies and rivalries, deceived by false teaching, or defiled by immoral conduct. These things are acts of sacrilege; they effectively destroy the church, for they destroy its unique identity as the holy people of God indwelt by the Spirit of God. "If anyone destroys God's temple, God will destroy him; for God's temple is sacred, and you are that temple" (1 Cor 3:17).

Question 9. Not only are your leaders yours, says Paul, but all things are yours, including the world or life or death or the present or the future. It is almost an incredible statement, but the reason for it is plain. All things are ours because we are Christ's and Christ is God's (1 Cor 3:23). As in Romans 8:17, we are "heirs of God and co-heirs with Christ." So what belongs to him belongs to us if he is ours.

Similarly, I doubt if pastors and church elders are wise to use the possessive adjective in relation to the church and refer to "my church," "my people," "my congregation." They do not belong to us, nor do we have any proprietary rights over them. It would be entirely biblical for them to refer to us as their ministers. But when we speak to them, it would be more modest to allude to them as "the people we have been called to serve." For we are their servants; they are not ours!

Questions 10-11. Use these questions to help your group take an honest look at the way Christian leaders are championed in their own settings. Some may want to voice changes they hope to make in the kind of attention they draw to themselves as leaders—or to other leaders they respect.

We must not, however, define the church in terms of its leaders but rather define leaders in relation to the church. We must also renounce secular views of the church as a merely human institution like any other corporate body, with human leaders wielding human authority and being treated as celebrities. All that has to go.

In their place we need to develop a godly view of the church as a unique community unlike any other: the redeemed and the covenant people of God. In this community, ministers give humble service. There is no boasting about human beings, but all boasting is directed to God the Holy Trinity: to God the Father, who alone gives growth to the seed; to God the Son, who alone is the foundation of the church; and to God the Holy Spirit, who alone indwells and sanctifies the church. So "no more boasting about men!" (1 Cor 3:21), but "let him who boasts boast in the Lord" (1 Cor 1:31).

Study 8. Keeping a Clear Conscience. 1 Corinthians 4:1-7.

Purpose: To cultivate a clear conscience in our leadership and our response to other leaders.

Question 1. This is an important (and difficult) question. Part of the difficulty is that these relationships are not linear and therefore do not fit well into a chart or reporting structure. The text clearly shows that Paul sees himself as a servant of Christ and therefore reports to God ("It is the Lord who judges me" [1 Corinthians 4:4]). But Paul has already said in 1 Corinthians 3:21 that he and the other leaders "are yours." Leaders are God's gifts to the church and therefore a part of it; these people are not necessarily the bosses of the church but the church's teachers—under the authority of God.

To complicate matters further, Paul says later in the letter (1 Cor 9:19) that he is also their servant with God-given responsibilities. Because of these shifting nuances, the relationships are difficult to chart, but the difficulty itself will help group members understand the complexity. These relationships are foundational to the rest of the study, so it is worth spending some time (and creativity) sorting them out.

Regarding the meaning of Paul's use of the phrase "servants of Christ" (1 Cor 4:1), Leon Morris comments: "[The Greek term] originally meant an 'underrower', i.e. one who rowed in the lower part of a large ship. From this it came to signify service in general, though generally service of a lowly kind ('subordinates', NEB), and subject to direction. The preachers are also *those entrusted with the secret things of God. Those entrusted with* translates *oikonomoi*, a terms which refers to the person who supervised a large estate. . . . Unless he was to be a slave to his slaves, a rich landowner had to find someone to do the routine work of running the estate. This deputy . . . held a responsible position; he was set over others and directed the day-to-day affairs. But he was subject to a master and was often a slave. Then in relation to the master he was a slave, but in relation to the slaves he was the master" (Morris, *1 Corinthians*, p. 75).

God's "mysteries" or "secret things" (1 Cor 4:1) are of course his revealed secrets. They are truths hitherto concealed but now revealed, truths known only by revelation. These revealed truths relate to Christ, his salvation, and the incorporation of Jews and Gentiles on equal terms in the body of Christ. Of these revealed truths, now contained in the New Testament, the apostles were the original stewards or trustees (cf. 1 Cor 2:10).

Question 4. Verses 1-4 will be helpful in sorting out these apparent contradictions. Paul (and other Christian leaders) is "entrusted" with a special mission from God. The primary responsibility of Christian leaders is to "prove faithful" in the discharge of that trust—with God as their judge. "It is the Lord who judges me" (1 Cor 4:4). Paul's pastoral responsibility to the church at Corinth included the unhappy task of confronting their sin and pointing them toward godly living. His mission (from God) was, in part, to judge and to reprove them with the goal that these Corinthian Christians would be fully reconciled to God—not only in their faith but in their practice of that faith. A natural response from the Corinthians would be to complain that Paul was judging them, even though he did not want them to pass judgment on him. This is not a case where Paul was flaunting the very laws he was announcing, but it was an explanation that his role as a leader, under God's judgment, required him to confront the Corinthians' sin. Today's pastors and other church leaders sometimes face the same dilemma—and are often roundly criticized for it. It is comforting to know that ultimately God will judge—he is the boss in such things.

Questions 5-6. This whole passage (1 Cor 4:3-7) emphasizes one main point, namely, that ministers of Christ (whatever form their ministry may take) are accountable to Christ for their ministry. Of course, we must listen to human criticism, however painful it may be—especially if it is untrue, unfair or unkind—but ultimately we are responsible to Christ. Fortunately, he is a more just and merciful judge than any human being, committee, council or synod.

On the one hand it is a comforting thing to be accountable to Christ; on the other hand it is challenging, for his standards are high and holy. And though much of a pastor's work is unseen and unsupervised by human beings, we are always in his presence. And we shall never grow slack or careless if we remember that he is watching us and that one day we will have to account to him.

Question 7. What is the difference between a clear conscience and innocence? Even though Paul could name himself as the chief of sinners (1 Tim 1:15), here in his ministry to the Corinthians, he was innocent of wrongdoing in his teaching. Paul had eloquently proclaimed that "All have sinned and fall short of the glory of God" (Rom 3:23), and he did not exempt himself from the need for salvation through Christ's death and resurrection. So he was not innocent (none of us are), but his conscience was clear because he was currently obeying God's call to confront, teach and care for the spiritual well-being of the Corinthian church.

The Corinthians may have had trouble distinguishing the difference between having a clear conscience and being innocent, but Paul reminded them that this was not their responsibility. "It is the Lord who will judge me." What are practical ways for a Christian leader to keep a clear conscience? Much will depend on the temptations unique to each individual— and a wise leader will deliberately confront these. Typical practices might include accountability partners, regular personal prayer and holy reading, listening compassionately to complaints and intentionally resolving personal conflicts (but not being leveled by them), glass doors in counseling rooms and offices, nurturing healthy family times, getting enough rest and refreshment, meeting obligations in a timely manner, keeping promises, practicing truth-telling, etc.

Study 9. Cultivating a Gentle Spirit. 1 Corinthians 4:8-21.
Purpose: To appreciate and cultivate love and gentleness in leadership.
Question 2. Let your group visualize their way through this paragraph, creating the various word pictures in their minds and voicing them to each other. They might come up with something like this: "In 1 Corinthians 4:8-13, the theater is packed with excited crowds. Event follows event throughout the day. Then, as the grand finale, criminals are either thrown

to the lions or forced to fight with gladiators." Paul's second metaphor was that of the kitchen. At the end of verse 13 he used two unusual expressions that had a somewhat similar meaning in the Greek. The "scum of the earth" was derived from a Greek word that means "to clean thoroughly," and seems to refer to sweepings off the floor; the "refuse of the world" seems to refer to scrapings from a dirty pot. Both alluded to the filth that one would get rid of through the sink or the gutter. Next Paul described some of his physical privations and persecutions (vv. 11-13). He and the other apostles had been treated brutally, but Paul knew the teachings and example of Jesus; he did not retaliate.

Question 3. Allow your group to consider principles growing from these metaphors; several seem fairly certain. Among them Paul was deliberately contrasting himself with the smug security and self-satisfaction of the Corinthian Christians. *Already,* he wrote, with more than a touch of sarcasm. Twice he used the "already" of a realized eschatology. But everything for them was "already"; there was no corresponding "not yet." Already they were eating and drinking and reigning, thinking that they had reached the top. Paul wished he could join them in the celebration. But he knew that the path to true glory is suffering. It was for Jesus; it is for his followers too. They had forgotten the cross. If the Corinthians were kings, the apostles were like criminals condemned to death. From these and similar observations, create general principles of Christian leadership: "A Christian leader should/is/will expect . . ."

Question 8. If you are leading a group, ask your group to pause at this point for silent self-examination. Then invite honest responses to the question. Many (most) Christians are called to be "spiritual parents" or mentors to someone. This is not just a verbal teaching situation; our followers will model us long before and after they hear us. And they won't hear us for long if they realize that they can't safely imitate us. Our actions will have made our leadership hollow. Christian leaders are called to high moral, ethical lives. Without lived-out Christianity worthy of imitation, our words of spiritual "wisdom" will likely cause more harm than good.

John Stott is known worldwide as a preacher, evangelist and communicator of Scripture. Stott has written many books, including Basic Christianity *and* The Cross of Christ. *This study guide is based on his book* Basic Christian Leadership.